Simple Solutions

Horse Safety

By Elizabeth Moyer
Illustrations by Jean Abernethy

For stable & saddle

BOWTIE
P R E S S®

A Division of BowTie, Inc.
Irvine, California

Lesley Ward, *Consulting Editor*

The horses in this book are referred to as *she* and *he* in alternating chapters unless their sexes are apparent from the activities discussed.

Library of Congress Cataloging-in-Publication Data

Moyer, Elizabeth.
  Horse safety / by Elizabeth Moyer ; illustrations by Jean Abernethy.
    p. cm. — (Horse illustrated simple solutions)
  ISBN 978-1-933958-24-8
  1. Horsemanship—Safety measures. 2. Horses—Handling—Safety measures. I. Abernethy, Jean. II. Title.

SF309.M69 2008
798.2—dc22   2007044677

BowTie Press®
A Division of BowTie, Inc.
3 Burroughs
Irvine, California 92618

Printed and bound in Singapore
10 9 8 7 6 5 4 3 2

CONTENTS

Safe Horsemanship

As far as some people are concerned, one end of the horse kicks and the other end bites. But knowledgeable equestrians understand "horse sense"—how horses think and react—and they know how to work safely around both ends of a horse.

If you enjoy equestrian activities, it is important to learn and follow safe horse handling and management procedures. Even experienced horse people need to remember to be vigilant about maintaining safe habits. Few things are more heartbreaking than an accident that could have been avoided.

Because of their size and strength, all horses are capable of causing injury. Even the gentlest horse might accidentally stomp

on your foot. There is inherent risk in all equine activities, but practicing safe horsemanship minimizes the risk of harm.

Despite their size and strength, horses startle easily and can be quite fragile and prone to injury. If there is a needle in that proverbial haystack, odds are a horse will find it and step on it, resulting in a puncture wound. Maintaining safe conditions provides an environment that minimizes the possibility of injury.

Equine Instincts

Like many prey animals, horses have a strong flight instinct; when they perceive danger, their first instinct is to run away from it. If running is not an option or the horse is startled, then she might resort to other defenses, such as kicking out.

Because horses prefer to outrun a threat, they need to be able to detect danger as early as possible. That's why they maintain constant awareness of their surroundings, and they notice and react to changes. Loud noises, mysterious rustling sounds, sudden motion, and anything that looks different or unusual will get a horse's attention and, quite likely, cause her to spook.

A horse can be desensitized to different objects, sounds, and situations if you gradually introduce the horse to these items until she no longer perceives them as scary or threatening. As horses gain experience and begin to trust their handlers to keep them safe, they can become less reactive to scary stimuli. Individual temperament also plays a role: some horses are naturally more timid or confident than others. However, there can be no guaran-

tee that the most steady, or "bombproof," horse won't be startled at some point. Never forget that a horse is a horse. No matter how puppy-dog-like a horse acts, it is not safe to treat a horse like a large dog—or a human, for that matter.

To move safely around horses without startling them, it is important to be aware of their blind spots. Having large eyes situated on the sides of their heads enables horses to see all around them—nearly 360 degrees. Although their eyesight is adapted to see danger on the horizon, horses have blind spots right in front of their noses and directly behind them.

Horses also have keen hearing. The position of a horse's ears tells you a lot about where her attention is directed and also expresses her emotional state.

Reading Your Horse's Mood

Here is a quick guide to detecting some basic equine emotions and states of mind:

Alert: ears pricked forward, head up, eyes wide, nostrils flared, tail raised, muscles tense

Attentive: ears flicking back and forth, or one ear forward and one ear back

Aggressive

Angry: ears pinned back flat against the head; snaky neck and head movement; bared teeth and open mouth; tight, pinched look around the mouth and nostrils; tail swishing; leg lifted, threatening to kick

Frightened: head up, whites of eyes visible, tail wringing or tensely clamped

Relaxed: head and neck lowered, ears to the side, eyes calm, mouth relaxed;  may lick or chew; lower lip may droop

The more time you spend around horses, the more adept you will become at reading them.

Relaxed

Fearful

Safe Horse Handling

Follow safe handling procedures when leading, grooming, and being around horses in general. From what you wear to how you approach your horse, safety on the ground is very important, yet some horse people get careless about it.

Being Properly Attired

Wear sturdy boots when working around horses. Sandals or flip-flops are not appropriate barn footwear. And although sneakers are comfy, they won't give you much protection either.

Avoid dangling earrings and other jewelry that might catch on something. The same goes for loose, draping clothes.

Don't forget about sun protection. If you don't want your hide to look like old leather, slather on the SPF.

It's a good idea, too, to have work gloves handy to avoid splinters, blisters, and rope burn.

Approaching a Horse

When approaching a horse, avoid coming upon him abruptly in any of his blind spots. Approach from the side or at an angle so he can see you coming.

Talk to the horse first so he knows you are there. If the horse is in the back of his stall or pen, wait for him to turn around and acknowledge you, then approach him. Take note of his demeanor; if he seems irritable or fearful, approach with caution.

If all is well, continue talking to the horse, and as you go up to him, place your hand on his body so he can keep track of your whereabouts. Loud or shrill tones tend to make horses jumpy, so talk to your horse in a calm, friendly, and level tone to inspire confidence. Make your movements smooth and deliberate because horses are good at sensing uncertainty or fear in your demeanor. Even if you aren't confident, you need to act like it to reassure your horse.

Leading the Way

Secure your horse with a halter so he can be led or tied. To catch and halter the horse, put your lead rope over his neck so you can grasp it in a loop to hold him if he moves away. Once the halter is buckled on, remove the lead rope from his neck. Most horses are accustomed to being handled primarily from the left side, a custom that dates back to cavalry tradition.

Standing at your horse's left shoulder, hold the lead rope in your right hand, eight to ten inches below his chin. Fold the extra lead rope in your left hand so it doesn't drag on the ground where you or the horse could step on it. Fold the lead rope rather than holding it in a loop, which could tighten around your hand. Never wrap the lead rope around your hand or fasten it anywhere on your body. If the horse were to pull away suddenly, you would be trapped and perhaps even dragged. For the same reason, do not lead your horse by the halter alone; your fingers could get stuck in the halter. Always use a lead rope.

When leading your horse, position yourself at his shoulder for optimal control and safety. He should walk willingly beside you, while respecting your space. Keep about a foot between you. The horse should not crowd you, pull ahead, or lag behind. If you need to correct the horse, use short tugs on the lead rope, as opposed to a steady pull. Your horse can lean into a steady pull, and that's a tug of war you're not likely to win.

Working Safely Around Horses

In the stall or other confined area, be aware of your position so you can't get pinned between the horse and a solid object. When releasing a horse in his stall, turn him so he faces the door; then, you can exit safely without putting yourself in a position where you might get kicked or stepped on.

As you work around your horse, talk to him and keep your nearest hand on him so he always knows where you are. You'll also be able to feel any tension in his body and have a little advance warning of his movements. Keep your body close to your horse's—this is the safest place for you to be. As you move around him, stay pressed close against him while minding where your feet are in relation to his. Try to keep your feet par-  allel to your horse's body to avoid being stepped on.

You can move around the hindquarters safely in this manner. If the horse kicks out and you are right up against him, you'll just get a little bump. If you are standing an unsuspecting few feet behind, you'll be in perfect range to receive the full power of the blow.

Do not pass under the neck of a horse, tempting as it may be to take this shortcut. He's apt to startle because he can't see you there. If he moves forward, you could get stepped on or knocked over.

Never sit or kneel on the ground by a horse's feet. If the horse moves suddenly, you won't be able to get up and out of the way in time. Crouch down if you need to reach something in a low place, and remain on the balls of your feet so you can spring out of the way if necessary. Remember also to never set your hand on the ground, or you risk getting your fingers stomped.

Be careful when grooming or touching your horse around his sensitive areas. Typically, the belly and flanks are ticklish spots for horses.

Finally, take care in feeding treats to your horse. Some horses get pushy and nippy if they habitually receive hand-fed treats. If this is the case with your horse, put all treats in your horse's bucket. If your horse is able to remain polite while taking treats from your hand, hold your palm out flat to avoid having your fingers munched by mistake.

Tying the Safe Way

Tying your horse is a routine part of grooming and tacking up, among other activities. While your aim is to tie securely to avoid the hazard of a loose horse running amuck, it is also important to be able to free a horse quickly if necessary.

You can accomplish this with a quick-release knot (see page 25) or by using special panic snap attachments, which stay fastened during normal use and release under additional strain during an emergency. Other considerations for tying safety are having safe surroundings and a suitable method of tying.

Most horses will safely stand tied. However, some horses have not been taught to tie properly, have had a traumatic experience

with tying, or have developed bad habits such as pulling back
when tied. In these cases, the horse will need to be retrained to tie.

What to Tie With

Tie with a halter and a lead rope. Avoid the slippery nylon styles, as they often won't hold a knot well. Avoid flat nylon and leather leads because they do not release easily and can get stuck, even when tied in a quick-release knot. Do not tie with a stud chain or chain shank, as these could injure your horse.

Never tie a horse by the reins. Although the old westerns show cowboys wrapping the reins around a hitching post, this is extremely risky. If the horse pulls back while tied by the reins, the bit can injure her mouth, and she'll probably break the reins.

Elastic ties are also a hazard. If they snap under stress, they'll create a slingshot effect, and the metal snap on the end could cause a serious injury to a horse or person.

The Quick-Release Knot

Step One: Put the free end of the lead rope around your hitching post or through a tie ring.

Step Two: Pass the free end of the lead rope around the part of the rope that is attached to your horse, forming a circle.

Step Three: Take the free end again, double it up, and pass the folded rope through the circle formed in step two.

Step Four: Pull down on the folded loop to snug up the knot. The knot comes undone in an instant with a simple tug on the loose end.

The ideal height to tie a horse is at withers level, with enough slack in the rope that she can hold her head in a normal position. If tied too low or with too long a rope, the horse might step over

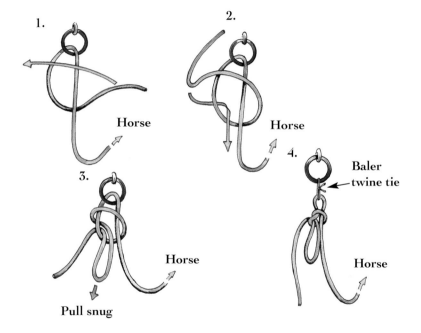

1.

Horse

2.

Horse

3.

Horse

Pull snug

4.

Baler twine tie

Horse

or pass under the lead rope and get tangled up. If tied too high or with too short a rope, the horse will be uncomfortable, and some horses may panic at the constraint.

Hitching Post or Rail

Tie your horse to a solid, immovable object that cannot break off. If you are using a hitching post or rail, the posts must be sunk deep enough that a horse cannot pull them up if she backs up.

Safety Loop or String

As an extra precaution, you may tie a loop of baling twine around the hitching post or tie ring and tie your quick-release knot to this loop. In an emergency, the baling twine should break and release the horse even before a panic snap gives — or if you can't undo the quick release knot in time.

Cross Ties

Cross ties secure a horse from both sides, keeping the horse centered in the tying area so it is easier for you to work around her. Cross ties may be set up in an aisle or a stall. One end of each cross tie clips to a side of the halter, and the other end clips to a tie ring at the wall.

Your cross tie setup should incorporate a quick release option. Typically, the panic snap on a cross tie attaches to the horse's halter. The other end of the cross tie is fastened at the wall.

If you must lead a horse down an aisle where another horse is cross tied, have someone unfasten one side of the tie to let you

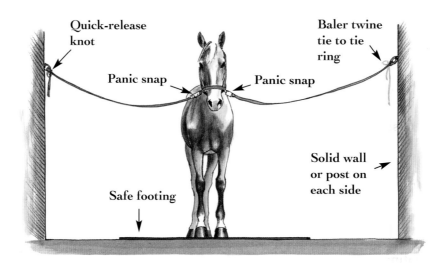

Quick-release knot

Baler twine tie to tie ring

Panic snap

Panic snap

Solid wall or post on each side

Safe footing

pass. Do not lead a horse underneath a cross tie. It is unsafe for two horses to be in very close quarters, and your horse risks getting tangled up while passing under the cross tie.

Safety Around the Barn

Make the barn a safe place for you and your horse. Cleanliness and fire prevention are top priorities. Your barn should also have a plan in place for responding to natural disasters that may occur in the area, such as wildfires, hurricanes, and earthquakes.

A Safe Haven

Footing around the barn should be designed to prevent slipping. For paved surfaces such as wash racks, tying areas, and sometimes barn aisles, some good nonslip options are textured concrete, rubber matting, and rubber pavers.

Hang up rakes and shovels when you are done using them to avoid creating a tripping hazard for you and your horse. Roll up hoses when you've finished filling water buckets. Regularly check stalls for protruding nails, splintered boards, and other sharp edges that could hurt a horse, and make any necessary repairs.

A loose horse is a danger to himself and others. If you have a horsey Houdini that is clever about opening gates and latches, you will have to take additional measures to foil your escape artist. Putting an extra clip through the latch or buckling a halter around the gate are some tactics you can use.

Be sure to store feed out of reach of horses. If presented the opportunity, horses will gorge themselves sick on rich grain and feed. Overindulging in feed can cause serious health problems

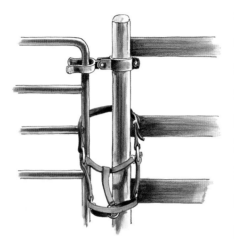

such as a ruptured stomach, colic (stomach pain), or laminitis (dangerous inflammation of the hooves). It's ideal to have a feed room with a door that can be fastened against loose equine lips. Store grain safely in the feed room in an airtight, rodent-proof latching container.

Good Housekeeping

Good management is important for horse health and barn safety. Stalls must be cleaned daily. Standing in manure and urine can

cause a horse's hooves to develop an infection called thrush, and ammonia fumes from urine buildup can affect a horse's respiratory health. Good manure management can also keep fly and internal parasite populations down.

Check water buckets, troughs, stock tanks, and automatic waterers daily, and clean them regularly to ensure that your horse always has access to clean, fresh water. Scrub away algae, and remove feed, manure, or other debris contaminating the water.

Maintaining clean water sources also discourages mosquitoes from breeding on the premises. Mosquitoes spread diseases, such as West Nile Virus, and pose a health risk to both horses and humans. Even a small amount of water that stagnates for four days or longer can serve as mosquito breeding grounds.

Visitors to the Barn

Visitors to your barn may not know how to behave around horses. To prevent guests from being injured, give them a quick introduction to horse safety and your barn rules. If you allow others to ride on your property, they should sign a liability release. (A lawyer can help you find an appropriate document that complies with your state's equine liability laws.) You may also need to protect yourself from the liability of uninvited guests approaching your horses.

Do not leave young children unsupervised around the barn. And if you bring your dog to the barn, Rover must be well behaved around horses; this may take some time and training on your part. Many boarding facilities recognize the risk of having dogs at the barn and either prohibit them or have specific rules in place.

Emergency Preparedness

As a horse owner, you'll need to plan and prepare to keep your horses and your barn—as well as any people on the premises— safe. Post the following emergency information in an easily visible place in your barn:

- name and contact information of barn owner
- property address and directions to give to all emergency responders
- backup emergency contacts: neighbors, relatives, and others who are familiar with you and your property
- name and contact information of veterinarian and farrier
- horses' names and descriptions
- telephone numbers of local fire and police departments

Fire Prevention

A barn fire is one of every horse owner's worst nightmares. Do everything you can to ensure that it never happens to your horse. Following are some preventive measures you can take to help keep your barn and your horses safe.

Every barn should be equipped with fire extinguishers; be sure to maintain yours regularly, and enforce a strict no-smoking policy around the barn.

Cleanliness also contributes to fire prevention. Keep the floor clear: sweep up loose hay and other debris that can create a fire hazard. Keep the overhead area clear as well: knock down cobwebs regularly, and be sure your lightbulbs are encased so that cobwebs cannot come into contact with them and ignite.

Store machinery and flammable substances a safe distance from the barn. If possible, store hay in a separate building. Hay storage should be covered and well ventilated to keep the hay dry and prevent mold—this is important because moldy hay can combust (and is unhealthy for horses to eat). Stack hay on pallets, with the bales in alternate directions, for good ventilation.

Many barn fires are caused by electrical equipment. Follow these tips to prevent an electrical fire in your barn:

- Don't overuse extension cords.
- Keep electrical cords out of reach of mouthy horses.
- Unplug cords when not in use.
- Keep rodents under control; these pests chew wires. Encase wiring so that it is rodent proof.

- Have wiring inspected by a licensed electrician.

Check with your local fire department for additional fire prevention tips.

Preparing for Natural Disasters

Disaster preparedness varies according to geographic region and climate. Wildfires, hurricanes, tornadoes, and floods are just a few of the natural disasters you might face in your particular area.

It's important to decide in advance where you will take your horses if you have to evacuate your property. In a time of disaster, a large fairground or equestrian center might be designated as a refuge for evacuees. It's a good idea to have several evacuation locations in mind in case one is full or is also at risk.

Teaching your horse to willingly load onto a trailer is an essential part of emergency preparedness. Even if trailering is not part of your regular activities, your horse needs to know how to load in case evacuation is necessary. If you don't own a trailer, prepare a list of haulers that you can call on in an emergency.

During some disasters, there is no time to evacuate. Depending on the type of disaster, the layout of your property, and the types of buildings you have, you may have to decide whether your horses are better off left in the barn or out in the pasture.

Be aware that even if your farm is not directly affected by a disaster, feed and other supplies may not be readily available in a disaster area. Keep a disaster preparedness kit on hand, with a first aid kit and adequate feed and water for all your animals.

Pasture Safety

Pasture turnout allows horses to live a more natural lifestyle than a stall allows. Out in pasture, they have the opportunity to move about and graze constantly, which is ideal for joint and digestive health. However, keeping a pasture environment safe requires planning and constant vigilance.

Safe Fencing

Keeping your horses in their pasture is a top safety concern. Loose horses out on the road are in grave danger and also create a hazard to motorists. An open gate is a significant pasture hazard that can be avoided. Always close gates behind you, and impress

upon others the importance of checking and double-checking that a gate is securely closed. Invest in a high-quality gate with a secure latch that horses can't open.

Appropriate, well-maintained fencing should contain your horse and pose the lowest risk of injury possible. The best choice for safe fencing depends on the type of horses behind it. Young horses are apt to be rambunctious and need safe, sturdy fencing. Foals, because of their small size, need fencing they can't roll under. Stallions are more aggressive and need higher, stronger fencing.

There are many types of horse-safe fencing materials to choose from, including traditional wood board, PVC, no-climb wire mesh, and various types of electric wire and tape. Barbed wire is never an acceptable choice for horse fencing. The consequences of a horse tangling with barbed wire are disastrous. This fencing was developed for cattle, whose hides are considerably thicker.

Whatever type of horse fencing you choose, keep it in good condition to ensure your horse's safety. Walk the fenceline of your pasture regularly to look for hazards and make repairs. Check for loose, cracked, or damaged boards and protruding nails. If you have electric fencing, it's especially important that you trim overgrown weeds that can cause short circuits. You must also maintain the voltage, tighten wires, and check for short circuits.

General Pasture Hazards

In addition to your regular fencing maintenance, check your pasture for hazards. Walk the pasture regularly, checking for rocks

that have worked their way up from the soil and animal burrows that could pose a hazard to horses.

Your pasture should not be a dumping ground for rusty old machinery and equipment. Find storage away from your horses.

Toxic plants are another pasture hazard. Check with your county agricultural extension agent if you are unsure about which toxic plants are common in your region. Some of the deadliest plants are oleander, yew, and foxglove. Other toxic plants include red maple, yellow star thistle, water hemlock, and locoweed.

In Good Company

Every herd of horses has a pecking order, from the dominant boss horse down to the subordinate herd members at the bottom of the totem pole. A dominant horse employs aggressive behaviors to keep lower-ranking herd members from overstepping their bounds. These behaviors include baring teeth, pinning the ears back, head slinging, striking, squealing, kicking, and biting.

Keeping compatible groups of horses pastured together reduces the risk of skirmishes and injuries. Some horses will just never get along; it is best to separate aggressive horses before they seriously injure one another. And bringing a new horse into an established herd upsets the hierarchy, so make careful introductions. It is best to introduce the horses across the fence first, keeping them in adjacent pastures before bringing the newcomer in.

Handling Pastured Horses

It can be tricky to remove your horse from a herd safely. You may need to carry a whip to keep more aggressive horses at a distance while you catch your horse. Hold the whip out as an extension of your arm, giving the horse a visual cue to stay out of your space.

Never carry treats or grain into a herd, or you could get mobbed by pushy horses.

If you must leave a halter on your horse to catch her, it should be a leather halter or a specially designed breakaway halter that will release if it gets caught on something.

Some horses get excited when being turned out and might kick out or bolt off. Work on training your horse to stay calm when you are turning her out. To stay safe, follow these steps when releasing your horse: Lead her through the gate and turn her back around so she is facing the gate. Close the gate and make her stand quietly for a moment; then slip her halter off and release her, being careful to keep your fingers free of the halter as the horse moves away from you.

Safety in the Saddle

Falling off is a part of riding that may be inevitable, but there are steps you can take to minimize risk and keep yourself as safe as possible.

Safe Riding Apparel

From head to toe, safe riding apparel items include a helmet, a body protector, and riding boots with flat soles and low heels.

Helmets

Helmets have been proved to reduce head injuries in equestrian accidents. The inner padding and outer materials are designed to absorb impact. Riding helmets should be approved by ASTM International (formerly called the American Society for Testing and Materials) and the Safety Equipment Institute (SEI); this approval is indicated on a label inside the helmet. This label verifies that the helmet has been tested and proved to meet a standard of safety for equestrians.

Some riding hats resemble riding helmets but do not offer any protective qualities. These riding hats are usually labeled Items of Apparel Only.

ASTM/SEI-approved helmets are required at many equestrian facilities and in certain competitive events, but often the decision to wear a helmet is a matter of personal choice. Make it a habit to wear your helmet during every ride, every time, with no exceptions. Accidents can happen to any rider, on any horse, at any time—even on the most leisurely ride, at a walk. Even the calmest horse can spook suddenly or take a misstep.

To get the full protective benefit of wearing a helmet, the helmet must fit properly. Many helmets feature adjustable fit systems to help you get just the right fit. These systems may include pads or a dial that tightens and loosens the fit.

Fit Test 1: Bend forward at the waist with the chinstrap unfastened; the helmet should stay on your head.

Fit Test 2: Wearing the helmet level on your head, place one hand on top of the helmet and wiggle it back and forth. Your eyebrows should move slightly.

Here are some additional fit tips:

- Wear your helmet level, not tipped backward or forward on your head.
- Adjust and fasten the harness correctly. The harness should touch your jawbones when the chinstrap is fastened.
- Fasten the chinstrap securely. It should be as snug as possible without sacrificing comfort. If the chinstrap is too loose, the helmet will be ineffective.

Replace your helmet after it receives impact in a fall, even if it isn't visibly damaged. The internal shock-absorbing properties may have been compromised by the impact. Do not store your helmet in a hot car either, as heat can break down the materials and weaken their protective qualities.

Body Protectors

Protective vests, or body protectors, are an additional safety item available for equestrians. Body protectors are most commonly worn for jumping activities, especially for rigorous cross-country jumping.

Boots

Proper footwear for riders features a low heel designed to keep the foot from sliding all the way through the stirrup and getting stuck. This "heel stop" keeps you from being dragged in the event of a fall. Your boots should also have flat soles. The work boots that you wear around the barn are probably too bulky to ride in and could get stuck in the stirrups because of their heavy tread.

Safe Tack

Make sure your tack is in good condition and properly adjusted before you mount up. Leather tack must be regularly cleaned and conditioned to stay strong, supple, and safe. Dry, cracked, or moldy leather is weak and could break. Stitching can come loose or rot. Before each ride, inspect your tack, especially key stress points on reins, stirrup leathers, billet straps, girths or cinches, and latigo leather. If you find damage, do not take a chance by using that tack; have it repaired, or replace it if necessary.

A slipping saddle is a common tack-related mishap that can be easily prevented. Check your girth (or cinch) before mounting and again a few minutes into the ride. (Some horses blow their sides out as the girth is initially being tightened, so it is important

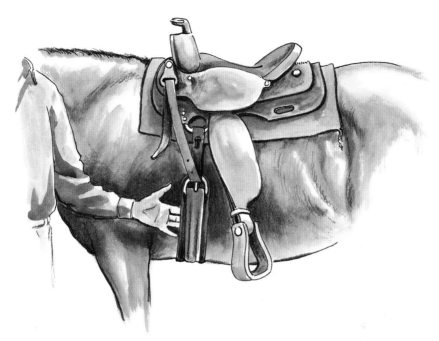

to recheck.) The girth should be snug, with just enough leeway to fit a few fingers underneath.

Many accidents happen when a rider's foot gets hung up in the stirrup during a fall, resulting in the horse dragging the rider. There are many safety stirrups designed to release the rider's foot.

English saddles feature a safety catch on the stirrup bar, where the stirrup leathers are hung on the saddle. The catch should be left in the open position, so the leather will release from the saddle in a fall.

With English saddles, you should put up your stirrups when you're not mounted so they don't bang into the horse's sides or get caught on anything. To run the stirrups up, grasp the bottom of the leather, slide the stirrup iron up to the top on the back half of the leather, and tuck the entire leather through the stirrup iron to secure it.

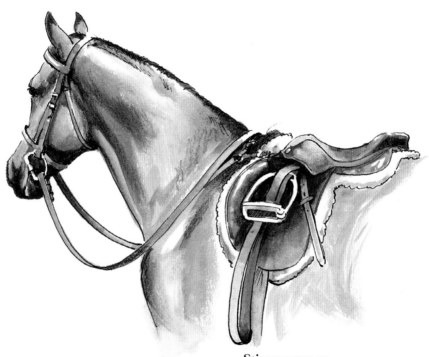

Stirrups run up

Safety in the Arena

Following proper arena etiquette is not only polite but also maintains the safe flow of riding traffic in an enclosed space and helps prevent collisions. Common sense, awareness of others, and good communication also go a long way toward maintaining a safe, productive riding environment. Practices may vary at different facilities, but here are some basic rules of the road for sharing the arena with others:

- In some arenas, it is customary to call "gate" or announce your intention to enter the arena.
- Horses traveling in different directions should pass left shoulder to left shoulder.
- Slower traffic generally stays to the inside.

- Faster gaits have the right of way. For example, a horse that is walking would yield to horses working at a trot or a canter.
- If it is unclear who will yield, call your intentions; for example, call "rail" if you intend to take the rail.
- Come into the center to halt, mount or dismount, adjust stirrups, and so on.

Safety on the Trail

Trail riding is one of the most popular pursuits on horseback. Whether it's just you and your horse or a group of friends riding out, here are some tips for safe and happy trails.

Before setting out, always tell someone where you are going and what time you expect to return. Carry a cell phone, and keep it on your body rather than in a saddlebag, in case you and your horse part company. Pack a simple first aid kit to deal with emergencies on the trail such as a lost shoe or a bleeding wound.

When riding in a group, following trail etiquette helps ensure a safe ride for everyone. Maintain a safe distance between horses. Some horses don't like to be crowded and might kick. When riding single file, one horse length between horses is the rule of thumb. However, if you lag too far behind the group, your horse may become upset at being left behind.

Don't pass without permission or come up suddenly on another horse—this could startle the other horse and set off a chain reaction. If your group includes riders of mixed ability levels, set the pace of the ride to the least experienced rider in the group. Trot or canter as a group, and make sure all riders are prepared for the change of pace. If you plan to stop, first raise your hand to signal riders behind you; this way, you will avoid causing a pileup.

Safety with horses encompasses many aspects—from being savvy in the saddle to keeping a safe environment back at the barn. It may seem like a lot to remember, but with consistent practice, safe horsemanship will become second nature. And by following safe horsemanship practices, you're sure to enjoy the time spent with your horse.

About the Author

Elizabeth Moyer is the editor of *Horse Illustrated* magazine, an award-winning title and one of the nation's largest equine publications. She has been with the magazine since 1999. Prior to that, she worked in advertising. She is a horse owner and lifelong equestrian. She has sat in almost every type of saddle but is currently pursuing her interest in dressage.